**TEMPTATIONS
and
BETRAYALS**

the dramas
by
Michael J. Austin

Drama for the painter!

Michael

Temptations was first performed at Theatre Church, Bolton, on 29th March 1994 by Peter Moreton and directed by Colin Bean. Betrayals was first performed in the chapel of All Saints, London Colney on 12th March 1995 by Peter Moreton, Director Colin Bean.

These scripts are copyright. They cannot be performed nor reproduced in whole or part without the express written permission of the author. For details of performance fees please contact Palaver Productions, 2b Park Road, Manchester, M30 9JJ.

Acknowledgements

"Temptations" and "Betrayals" would not have been developed or presented without the encouragment, the enthusiasm and the argumentativeness of Peter Moreton, the actor and friend who first performed them and shared the adventure of putting them on around the country. Peter's contribution to their development cannot be over-emphasised. Thank you Peter.

Colin Bean who first directed both pieces is also now a friend and that is a tribute to the commitment he has shown to the pieces and to his enthusiasm for them.
Thank you Colin.

Thanks also to the friends whose response to the first reading and helpful criticism made Peter and I believe that we had something worth working on.
Thanks to our "angels" and the people who worked to get the first productions underway.

Finally thanks, as always, to Jane, Henry and Catherine, my family, who tolerate my crazy schemes, help get them underway, and sometimes suffer the consequences.
Thanks you lot.

First published February 1996 by Palaver Publications
Copyright 1996 by Michael J. Austin
All rights reserved.

ISBN 0 9516767 1 7

DRAMAS

There is more
than one way
of creating
Icons.
There is patience
in the painter
putting paint
to plaster.
But then there
is our Way,
taking all that
makes us human
in word and
flesh shaping
into Time.
For these passing
moments,
Thanks.

*Dedicated to all who make theatre
especially Peter and Colin
and to my family.*

*"Betrayals"
remembers Michael
who also chose death.*

St. Matthew, 4.

THEN was Jesus led up of the spirit into the wilderness to be tempted of the devil.

2 And when he had fasted forty days and forty nights, he was afterward an hungred.

3 And when the tempter came to him, he said, If thou be the Son of God, command that these stones be made bread.

4 But he answered and said, It is written, Man shall not live by bread alone, but by every word that proceedeth out of the mouth of God.

5 Then the devil taketh him up into the holy city, and setteth him on a pinnacle of the temple,

6 And saith unto him, If thou be the Son of God, cast thyself down: for it is written, He shall give his angels charge concerning thee: and in *their* hands they shall bear thee up, lest at any time thou dash thy foot against a stone.

7 Jesus said unto him, It is written again, Thou shalt not tempt the Lord thy God.

8 Again, the devil taketh him up into an exceeding high mountain, and sheweth him all the kingdoms of the world, and the glory of them;

9 And saith unto him, All these things will I give thee, if thou wilt fall down and worship me.

10 Then saith Jesus unto him, Get thee hence, Satan: for it is written, Thou shalt worship the Lord thy God, and him only shalt thou serve.

11 Then the devil leaveth him, and, behold, angels came and ministered unto him.

TEMPTATIONS

Desert.
Dead
Sand.

Sand in my feet, my nose, my hair,
Sand in every crevice, everywhere.
Sand lifted up
running through the fingers.
Desert.
Dead
Sand.

Outside
Inside

Outside
The desert deception place.
What you see, not what you get.
Distance impossible to judge,
Place of mirage,
and False hope.
Day deception.
Deceiving in the heat.

Look at this place.
This sand place, shade less
sun, great ball burning
each grain hot
into baking,
making dry fire of footsteps,
hardly bearing
the deep heat,
conquering life's
attempt to live here.
Each day a flame
question against my life.

Days of it.
Forty days of it.
Slaking sun burns sun burn in my skin,
skin that soaks unnatural,
almost the death smell,
heat, almost too hard to bear.
Impossible to live here.

Then come the nights of it.
Out of day heat come the night cold wracks,
another extreme,
aching bones with cold,
deep cold to shiver
frozen into numb.

Every day a testing,
burning the soul as well as the skin.
Every night a trying,
testing the pain of it,
the pain of it mysterious,
yet fascinating.

Fascinating?

Yes. Without the fascination where would I be?
I would not be here that is certain.
For fascination drew me to the desert
Fascination brought me to John.
I came to John the Baptiser's desert
and he made me find my own.
For there in John's desert
I discovered that deep, deep down
there is desert in my heart.
I am missing something,
not doing something I should be doing somehow.
I have something to do in my life
and I must begin it now.
And if I do not begin it now then I shall be nothing;
I shall be as dead as this desert.

But, what answers are there here?
For forty days and nights I have tested myself
against this desert
but still
all I have is the knowledge
that somehow I must shape a future.

But what future?
Future's impossible to tell
except for the certainty
that while life is
not destroyed by the desert
there will be faces here
for life is exploration
in the desert
outside
inside.

Imagine
imagine and I almost see those future faces
sitting,
watching me here.

Hard for me to imagine though,
those future faces
for even my imagining
seems deception
until I choose a future.

And then what?
What are the faces of my choosing?
My choosing imagines futures
from my present.
My choosing shapes me
and other futures,
others
are shaped by my choosing.

But how to choose
when all the desert seems
is

Dead.
Dead sand.
Dead desert.

How to choose
when
the desert rings with the sound of the dead.
They do not rot here.
Their remains live on.
In the dry air their smell.
Dead patriarchs.
Dead prophets.
Dead mothers.
Dead children.

They all passed through this desert once.
Living their lives.
Marching their footprints into my present.
Imagining my face perhaps.
Living in their turn as I live now.
They put their footprints down, as mine go down now.
Only to be covered again by the sands.
Dead sands.
Covering the traces.
Desert.
Deserted.

Though some found God here.
God covenants,
binding themselves into laws,
laws for themselves,
laws for others,
and all the while the people were wanting earth things,
sand things perhaps.
And who can blame them?
Earth is all we know.
Gold glitters.
Lust is for life.
Only prophets want something else,
and prophets are always strange.

Will I be strange too?
Is that why I am here?
Deserted?
Thrust here by my own desert?
Heart aching with wonder,
wonder why I am here
among the dead?
Dead sand.
Desert.

Why am I here?
Where do I go back to?

In the beginning, they say,
there was death,
Herod slaughtered Innocents.
Did others die for me?
But I was innocent too,
a child,
not knowing death,
nor life hardly,
scarce born
yet somehow guilty of their deaths,
they say.
Burdened from the beginning
with death.

No wonder my parents went,
trying to escape the memory
of it perhaps.
Do I go back there then?
To my own half memories
of my beginning?

Do I try and remember again
desert fleeing parents,
heart beating terror of mother,
feeding the fear with the food;
half-remembering the running,
donkey, Egypt,

bone memories of slavery,
prejudice and the stranger?
Or do I come back later
to the hesitant return,
rediscovering roots,
Nazareth, discovering boyhood
among the tools, rules, and trade ways?
No desert there.
Only a holy family.

Holy?
Strange word that.
Cut off. Separate. Set apart.
We were none of those things.
We were in the midst,
in the carpenter's shop,
life coming to us for repairs.
Mend this. Make that.

And the wood.
Taking from the start the feel of it,
creation in the hands,
run the finger along the edges,
different feels,
different woods;
rough woods, bark stripped
ready for work;
the push pull sawing into shapes
rough edges,
ready to be plane pushed
into smooth, grain smooth,
good to touch.
Touching the tools too,
adze, saw, drill, plane,
hammer again,
tool testing,
finger feeling edges
for the sharp, edge perfect.

The sharp necessary, but needing care
in the handling, or the sharp cuts

into nicks, or worse —
thin lines surprised
into blood lines,
pain lines, mouth sucking
to stop the flow,
but all the while blood
part of the work,
not welcomed
but necessary.

Necessary too, the arm strong,
moulding muscles along with the wood;
the eye, sharp to see and estimate
cost and measure.

Not necessary perhaps
but lingering are the smells,
smells of the cedar, box, acacia,
pine dust swept into corners,
at the days end.

I go there in my memory.
I am back there now.
Back in the shop.
Make this. Mend that.
the hands rough again,
but not the heart,
for in the home were the hearts.
And truth is,
in the home
were God rules too,
God rules taken seriously,
and shared,
living not just saying,
and not without humour.

There was a joke once, —
Actually there were many,
word plays, fun things, stories,
smiles all part of it —
but this one I remember.

Zach went to see God.
When he got to God he asked him a question.
"Is it true God," he said, "that we Jews are your chosen
people?"
"Yes." says God.
"Well, do you think you could choose someone else for a change?"
"You think you could choose someone else for a change?"
The laughter rolled around the house for days,
became a private joke.
Choose someone else. Choose someone else.
Not my job. Choose someone else.

There's no laughter here.
Only the hollow laughing self mockery
of why am I here?
Is this some kind of joke?
The voice says,
If you had wanted to escape
you should never have gone to see John.
You could have gone on being the carpenter of Nazareth
if you'd not gone there.

So why did I go?
Oh I know everyone was going out to see him,
attracted by the idea that he might be one
of the old time prophets returned.
But what made me go out to his desert?
Was the idea that he might be holy too, too fascinating?
And if so, did I find the holy there,
lurching beneath his camel hair,
feeding on his locusts and wild honey,
wailing in the fierceness of his "Repent",
pouring in the waters of his baptism?
He was in the desert too.
Was that his own?
Or someone else's?

But go to his desert I did.
And then, to be honest,
all I found at the time was embarrassment.
I had wanted to sneak down,

be part of the crowd,
and then be like everyone else,
be baptised, and melt back into the crowd again.
But oh no, he singled me out, knew my history, knew me.
"You should baptise me," he said.
"You are special. You are God's chosen one."
"You need to baptise me," he said.
I went to sneak a look at his holiness
and I found holiness terrifying me.
"Go on. Baptise me." I pleaded.
"Don't impose your holiness on me.
I'm not sure I want it.
Let me be baptised
and sneak back to be the carpenter of Nazareth."

But I couldn't do it.
The baptism changed things.
The baptism changed things alright.

Once, perhaps in the carpenter's shop,
there was certainty,
life seemed mapped out,
holy hunger seemed excluded by the service of the moment.
But now,
How can I go back to Nazareth with "God-son" written in my head?
How could I return to be a carpenter with a kingdom at hand?

The Baptism has made me hungry.
My own desert is the hunger.

But that baptism told me something else too.
It told me there is a great hunger in others also.
So many souls in the desert.
And what did they go to see?
Not reeds shaking in the wind.
Not a man dressed in fine clothes.
No. They went to see someone they thought could feed them,
take away their hunger, and feed them.
And fanatic though he was he did feed them
or they would not have been baptised.

That wild man preaching took them outside the rules of religion,
took them away from the uncertain certainties
of those who claim to know,
and gave them the possibility of a new start.

In our Temple religion
all the scribes have is their scrolls, —
I see that now —
scrolls bound by tradition
and their attempts to explain
to a people whose
lives leap away from their pages.
But John took the past and reclaimed it.
He took all that had gone before and redeemed it,
gave the people a new dignity,
a new future, free for a while from the hunger.
No wonder they flocked to him in the desert.
Those are the things we all want.
And now their hungry hearts hang on my heart.
The baptism voice says,
"Be the God-son. Feed their hunger."

But how to do it? That is the question.
Can the desert here help me?
I came here to fast,
to fast and find answers,
but forty days,
forty days, forty nights,
and all I am left with is the hunger,
my hunger, and the burden of the hunger of others.
How can I feed this hunger?
How can I feed the hunger of others
when I can scarce feed the hunger of my own?

What is that?
The voice says,
Go back to the baptism.
Go back to the baptism?
Yes, the baptism told me something else too.
Hunger has power.
Hunger plants seeds of creation.

Hunger prompts.
Hunger moves.
Hunger drives.

And, O God I am hungry now!
Hungry body.
Hungry mind.
Hungry spirit.
Hungry.
Feed me please!
Let hunger have its power.
Look.
Let this stone be turned to bread.

Hunger power could do that couldn't it?
Faith hunger has always done such things.
I remember the stories of the Word.
I grew up on them.
They were given to me.
Part of my childhood.
Part of my tradition.
And those stories speak of faith hunger being fed.
Moses fed the children in the desert?
Faith hunger fed Judge Gideon and his army.
The faith hunger of Elijah and the widow was filled from an empty pot.
Why should I not do it now?

Let hunger power do the conjuring trick.
Let this stone be turned to bread.
Let the hunger be fed.
My faith is sufficient.
I claim food for myself.
I claim food for the hungry.
Let me be the Saviour of the hungry.
God knows, such a Saviour is needed
when women scratch at soil for seeds,
when children suckle dry breasts
and grow the bloated bellies that mock their hunger.

Why should I not be such a Saviour?
I will be the one who feeds them,
fills their bellies and feeds them,
and as I feed them so I will teach them,
teach them of the goodness of my God.
Look. See. How gracious the Lord is.
He fills you.
By me, the hungry shall be filled with good things.
Let this stone be turned to bread.
Let the hunger be fed.
Let hunger power do the conjuring.

But wait.
The dialogue begins again.
I want this and I don't want it.
I hesitate.
I came here to fast.
To live with the hunger for a while.
To fast and put myself with the hungry.
Should I end my fast with a faith trick?

What is bread without seed-planting,
seed-tending, seed harvesting?
What is bread without work, time, sweat, tears?
Could my easy bread satisfy?
Or would I always taste the stone beneath the bread?
Is comfort to be found so simply?
Or does comfort only come by bearing the pains,
taking the hard way,
enduring until the end?

And what if I fed others such stone bread?
They would see me as a Saviour, all right,
a Saviour of the belly full.
But could such a Saviour satisfy their need?
Or would stone bread comfort only stir their greed?

Perhaps there is another way to feed,
a way to feed with living bread,
a way to give life to the dead,

a way to feed body, heart and head.
If stone bread comfort would only leave stone dead,
then I must find another way instead.
Give us this day our daily bread.
And remember.
Remember a word!
Remember a word of the Holy Word.
"You do not live on bread alone
But by every word that comes from the mouth of God."
And what are those words?
Are they answer or question?
So often our Holy Word words are presented as answer —
obey and there shall be blessing,
respond and all shall be well, —
but are they not actually a question?
The Holy Word, is it not a word to talk to,
to talk to me, open-ended?
Is it not a dialogue to be entered,
not an answer but a question?
And what is its question now?

"You do not live on bread alone
But by every word that comes from the mouth of God."

Bread. Bread alone is not enough.
Bread may fill the body but the hunger will remain.
We live by the word that comes from the mouth of God.

And what is the mouth of God?
I am that mouth.
I am to be that word.
My fasting body shall be a bread that feeds.
I shall offer my body as a living bread,
not for an easy way,
not offering the comfort of stone bread,
but offering the struggle,
my struggle for holiness,
the struggle to sustain the wholly human.
I will try to go beyond the temporary hungers,
and address the holy hungers.
That will be a hard way I know.

They will mock me for my holy hunger.
They will call me irrelevant to the needs of the world.
But mine will be a way of holy hunger.
I shall take that way.
I shall take that way.

But wait.
Again I hesitate.
Should faith not be tested?
Back away from turning stones to bread
Back away from cheap comfort,
That is fine; that is honourable perhaps.
But what of the principle?
Can faith be faith without the test?
Does faith not grow in the testing?
Come!
Let me check this testing.

Come, Let me go to the faith place,
the Holy City.
Let me go to the holy temple.
And see the faith there.
Let me see the faith built into the very stones
of tradition, law rites making sacrifices
in faith, faith in praise,
faith in contrition,
faith for absolution offering
new starts, new beginning;
faith in prayers beseeching, hoping, entreating;
faith in the sacrifice.
And now let me stand here for a while
in this Holy Temple place,
and let me see the faith of others
and let me compare it with my own.

My faith has always been strong here.
So many times we have come,
all of us, the family,
mother, father,
extending outwards into our community.
We came for the rituals,

year by year,
ritual important to religion,
sacred dances,
trying to impose some order onto the confusion.
And, O I love these things.
The beards, the books, the special clothes,
ceremonies and processions.

When did they first really strike me I wonder?
Oh yes! Of course I remember.
When was it we came?
I must have been twelve or thirteen?
I was already in the carpenters shop.
I had seen life.
I had studied in the school.
I knew it all.
We had come for the Passover,
but the Passover was over when
I came to the Scribes here
and sat down with them and asked them questions
and slept on the hard floor
for more the following day.
Engrossed I was,
though the family had gone.

They were on their way back to Nazareth
but hurried back to find me.
They found me here,
here in this Temple.
When they found me my Mother was anxious,
angry with anxiety.
"Son, why have you treated us like this?" she asked.
But I knew.
I knew, like I know now.
"Why were you searching for me?" I asked.
"Did you not know that I had to be in my Father's house?"
I had the faith then and I have it now.
See how it compares with the faith of others.

Look the rich men come into the Temple,
fine dressed and fancy,
paying their bribes to God
in token of His blessing.
But can I blame them?
Is not even that gesture a token of some kind of faith?
But I do not need the bribery.
Oh no! I do not need that!

Look too at the merchants,
selling the unblemished goods for the sacrifices,
the thank offerings and the guilt offerings,
turning the courtyard into a market place
for trading in the sacred.
Point being, their pure produce actually works,
does actually meet the needs
the need to give thanks,
the need to be at-oned.
Their pure produce does its tricks
because the people buy and believe.
But I do not need to buy.

But look.
A widow comes and..... what now?
She offers her two pennies to the Temple.
All she has. I know it.
A futile gesture some might say.
Two pennies will make no difference
to her or to her temple,
neither to her because she already has the faith,
nor to the temple because the temple needs much larger gifts.
All she has is a gift of faith,
a simple reliance on God to survive.
Give away everything
and perhaps you gain the whole world.
Should I then, not test my faith by hers?
Should I then not trust God too like that?

Remember the baptism.
Remember the baptism.
You are God-son.

You are God-son, it said.
Why not test the faith you claim?
Why not throw yourself down from this high place?
Why not jump, jump in faith?

And remember a word,
Remember a word of the Holy Word.
"If you are God-son
He will put his angels in charge of you,
they will support you in their arms,
for fear you should strike your foot against a stone."

This Temple is a holy place.
God is surely here if he is anywhere,
why should I not test my faith in this holy place?
What a faith demonstration that would be?
Floating down on the wings of faith.
A miracle indeed.
People would flock to see such faith demonstrated.
There would be no limit to what such faith might do.
Such faith might even move mountains.
Such faith would compel belief,
move people to the mighty power of God.

Why not then?
I can do it. I know I can.
Why not test the faith I claim?
Why not throw myself down from this high place?
Why not jump, jump in faith?

Do I lack the courage, the faith,
or do I simply not believe?
The arguments are subtle,
but truth is, actually I do not believe in such a faith.
Faith must be tested. Yes.
Faith does grow by being tried.
But the testing must be God's, not mine.
Leaping must be a response to God's call.
I cannot test my own faith for then I worship myself.

The test is not to test.
"He will put his angels in charge of you,
they will support you in their arms,
for fear you should strike your foot against a stone"
but only when I am going in his paths,
walking in his ways.
Only then.

So remember!
Remember a word!
Remember the true word of the Holy Word.
"You are not to put the Lord your God to the test."
"You are not to put the Lord your God to the test."

And so I will not.

I will replace test with trust and walk away from this place.
Let others be temple leapers if they dare;
I shall be a faith leaper,
not looking for the guardian angels,
but looking to the God call,
the God call, "Be faithful, be faithful to the end."

It will not impress the sensation seekers, of course,
those looking for the latest quick thrill,
the latest trend, the latest thing.
They would have been far more impressed with the temple leap.
That might even have made me famous for a while.
But no regrets. I must be reconciled.

My way now will not impress them
for this is a way of quietness,
a way of contemplation,
a way of prayer that is contemplation,
a way of trying to discern the voice of God,
a voice at best only half heard.
On the steps of this temple I shall make my body a temple,
a temple not made with hands,
but made with my struggle of prayer.

But wait.
Wait a moment.
You will address the holy hungers, you say,
you will take the way of God-call.
But how do those break in?

How do those break in through the din of the human?
Come. I must look at this human.
Come let me climb away from this desert to the heights.
Come let me climb a very high mountain,

for mountains are places to see kingdoms,
and kingdoms are creations of the human,
and mountains are sometimes holy places.
Perhaps on this mountain I will see the way to break in.

Look then.
Look. What do I see?
I see the kingdoms of this world,
human worlds,
young women, old men, children,
old women, young men,
hopes, fears, struggle, joy,
delight, disappointment,
sometimes marked in faces,
sometimes marked inside;
I see the rich diversity of races,
graces in the faces,
strong in the black, the blond, the brown,
and the glory of them.
I see cultures with their own marks, own ways,
respected valued, traditions honoured,
and the glory there,
I see people breaking out of cultures,
finding new ways,
and the glory there.
I see the still, sitting at the fireside,
and their glory.
I see the restless, struggling with creation,
and their glory.
I see doctors caring for the sick,
philosophers, struggling for the truth,

dancers, shaping their bodies to the universe,
poets, shaping their words to the winds,
artists, working to bring beauty to expression.

I see them.
I see their glory, the glory of the human.
And is not this also the glory of God?
These kingdoms of this world,
are they not also his,
his creation?
These kingdoms, do they not belong to His kingdom?
Did the baptism not remind me that there was a kingdom at hand?
Then why not be a king?
I have been given the grace.
Is this not the way to feed the holy hungers?
Is this not the way to share the God-call?

My nation thought so once.
Were not our kings God-sons too?
What did the Psalmist say, the holy singer?
"I shall announce the decree of the Lord:
"You are my son," he said to me;
"this day I will become your father.
Ask of me what you will:
I shall give you nations as your domain,
the earth to its farthest ends as your possession." "

Our Kings were anointed as God-sons
to establish the good news,
to conquer with it and carry with it,
to lead the people in the way of peace,
to establish the law with justice.
And should I not take this cause?
Many are calling for it.
Zealots are creating revolution for it.
Even those struggling to live with the system
secretly, in their heart sense, desire it.
My people would rejoice in it.
It would restore their dignity;
restore their identity,
show them their God rules.

No longer subject to the rules of others
a God-son King could establish the God rules.
So, should not I, declared God-son in baptism,
use the gifts of that baptism to become a King,
a God-son in the line of David?
Will the nations of the world
and their glory become my glory,
become my dominion?
And then will my kingdom be God's kingdom
on earth as in heaven?
Like king David I shall follow the God-call.
Like king Solomon I shall address the holy hungers.
Perhaps the holy temple will be restored.
Perhaps the nations shall come to it and find their peace.
Perhaps.....
perhaps.....

Perhaps I should remember the old kings
and their corruption.
Created to worship God in the end they worshipped themselves,
Created to share the power of God in the end they worshipped
their own power.
In this king thinking,
what am I worshipping?
Oh the subtlety of temptation!
Oh the temptation to power.
Even now I am thinking of it.
Even now the very idea of it seduces me.
Power. Power.....
Power over men......
Power over women.....
And the lust there.
Power.....
If you will worship me.....

"All of these I will give you
if you will only fall down and do me homage."

Thus I become a Satan.
Thus we all become Satans.
Lusting for the power which belongs only to God,

and God has renounced it,
renounced it in love.

And so I say,
"Get behind me my Satan. Get out of my sight!"
Get behind me
for you are my past and now I am shaping a future.
I remember.
I remember a word.
I remember a word of the Holy Word.
"You shall do homage to the Lord your God
and worship Him alone."
You shall not worship power
or even the idea of power,
for the idea of power is lust,
and lust is the craving to be a god,
to exploit, manipulate the creation.
Power is for empowering
and I must give my power to others.

That is why I cannot be an earth king.
My kingdom, if I am to have any, will not be of this world.
My kingdom shall be a kingdom of the poor
worshippers in deed, a kingdom
of festivals at which true children reign,
where blind ones look at themselves
in mirrors, and love looks back at them.
In my kingdom deaf ears shall hear songs
of freedom, and dumb tongues shall speak
praise, for their voice suppressed
says the deep truth that life is broken
but worshipful.

I will not take kingdoms from above,
I shall make a kingdom from below.

So,
Make Clear!
My high Way shall be
a souls weighing Way,
weighing against my love
judgement.

What do I say then?
What do I say here?

I say,
in my way of love
judgement
I must begin with myself.
I must begin with the choices
I have made
and love them,
embracing their joy
and bitterness.
If I am to take my way.
I must embrace even my Satan;
taking the temptations,
that make me holy,
wholly human,
claiming them,
claiming them as mine,
saying,
Now Satan I have conquered you
beaten you with my love
In claiming you.

And I must love myself,
no longer relying on the love of others,
taking my own love
future to carry me through,
Wood worker become good worker,
God worker, with all
that is involved in that.
Boy become man
become God-son again.

And
I must love this desert,
for here I find the way to love others,
the way which declares,
I am to be poor too,
taking their way of suffering,
so that they may recognize me in that way.

And
My way will be known by them.
It will be known by children.
It will be known by the simple.
It will not speak the power languages of the rich,
their languages of exclusion,
but it will speak by way of story,
women will tell
my stories at their wells.
My language will be the language of the singer
writing on hearts,
of the clown, writing in joy,
of the speechless, speaking in signs.

And so tempter, myself,
I deny the cheap comfort way of stone bread,
I reject the cheap faith way of the test leap,
I renounce the power of the kingdoms.
So be gone subtle temptations
to alter my path,
they are the past
and all I have now is the future;
And here I define my way.
I say let the holy way,
the God way's Will be done.
For better or worse I take the cup of it.
I drink of its fullness.
I stretch out my arms to embrace it.

Oh hunger you are being satisfied.
Oh angels, you do minister to me.
Oh desert the miracle has begun —
for desert, I see your promise,
I see you begin to bloom,
to bloom with a crop for a harvest.
Desert you are not dead any more.
What was dead has come to life.
I take the life and embrace it.
I take bread and break it.
I take faith and live it.
I take my poor power and share it.

And so I must away.
The time is fulfilled.
The time is now.
I have a future.
The work must begin.
There is in deed a kingdom at hand.
So be it. So be it.
Let me begin
and end.

St. Matthew, 26.

36 ¶ Then cometh Jesus with them unto a place called Gethsemane, and saith unto the disciples, Sit ye here, while I go and pray yonder.

37 And he took with him Peter and the two sons of Zebedee, and began to be sorrowful and very heavy.

38 Then saith he unto them, My soul is exceeding sorrowful, even unto death: tarry ye here, and watch with me.

39 And he went a little farther, and fell on his face, and prayed, saying, O my Father, if it be possible, let this cup pass from me: nevertheless not as I will, but as thou *wilt*.

40 And he cometh unto the disciples, and findeth them asleep, and saith unto Peter, What, could ye not watch with me one hour?

41 Watch and pray, that ye enter not into temptation: the spirit indeed *is* willing, but the flesh *is* weak.

42 He went away again the second time, and prayed, saying, O my Father, if this cup may not pass away from me, except I drink it, thy will be done.

43 And he came and found them asleep again: for their eyes were heavy.

44 And he left them, and went away again, and prayed the third time, saying the same words.

45 Then cometh he to his disciples, and saith unto them, Sleep on now, and take *your* rest: behold, the hour is at hand, and the Son of man is betrayed into the hands of sinners.

46 Rise, let us be going: behold, he is at hand that doth betray me.

BETRAYALS

Stay.
Stay there disciples please.
Stay and keep awake awhile.
Though the wine and the night
send sleep into your eyes
I would have this time
go on longer,
For how many nights do you get
like this in a life?
Nights when soul disclosing
comes natural;
nights when friend can speak
to deep friend and say, "I am,
this is me"?

For this is where we are
tonight, and God,
it is good.

With the good
old ancestors we have
taken the old Passover
to renew our company
of friends.
We broke bread tonight,
held the cup tight
to look into the eyes
of shared memory,
where we came from,
where we have been, to be
word and action
signed into blood
brothers of remembrance.

So will you come
with me a way,
brothers of the special
memory, Simon,

James, John,
a little further
into the depths
and testing;
for here
in this Gethsemane
green garden, wine
press place, I know myself
pressed to the stone
hard questions
that will not move.
Yet …

The Garden
gives the question.
Always.

The garden gives true colour
— but not in the dark.

Beauty shows here
— but decays.

Life grows
— but dies.
(They bury in gardens!)

The life/death garden
cycle creates
The question
Questions me!

I do not want this question.
It raises things
I do not want raised up.
I want the good night
to continue

The garden was paradise
— and betrayal?

Is betrayal here
again? Who is betrayed?

The garden has the flower
— and the stone.

Though my heart might break
with the grief of it
Pick up the stone.

But wait here my three
disciples, a stones throw stay
For now I must pray!
I must find a way
to go beyond the adult
prayers of words manipulated
to get the God on our side.
I must find a way
back to the true prayer
that is the prayer of the child
before sleep, which asks in innocence
from the Papagod for love
and nothing else.
True prayer makes children
of us all, means love's
truth and nothing else,
and I must pray
because I must understand
some Truth
here in this garden
And there must be some
questions, for true
prayer questions
everything in the light
of Truth. Such prayer is hard
stone always, but necessary.

Am I prepared for this
if prayer is answered
with suffering as true
prayer so often is?

I am pressed
here tonight
to pray but find
myself afraid
of prayers answer.
Prayer is dangerous
and I begin to see things

I do not want to see. Yet
All I should say
here in this garden is
I love you men.

Not that I have not loved
the women.
They have always been there;
the mother love at the table,
feeding first foods, manners
mind and more. Then
there were sisters
growing into women
with husbands, and me
taking the father place
when father died.
Love managed things.

I remember too, girl teasing
in the village, before
beginning my way,
making the choices
that led me here
to this garden.
But even on the way
women have loved me

and been loved
by me, in the special way
of sex opposites,
shape attracting,
sense affecting,
round against my rigid
denial of the flesh
for spirit
Meaning ...
I loved the busy Martha
hustling affairs, cares, repairs.
I loved too the sister,
Mary of the stillness,
soul-mated to my still perhaps
but still denied me.
And the Magdalena.
She saw me seeing
her and the knowledge
grew that she knew me
too, wake enough to
wash my feet with ...
What? Recognition
of something I still
do not want to recognize. Yet

Sense stirs still in the memory
of that sensual anointing
and its possibilities.
How the religious ones disapproved of that!
They claimed their righteousness
in their concern for the poor
care for themselves
not her. And all I could
think of was wanting her
caring to continue.
Sister, you were more
than disciple then!
Yet I went no further.
Did you want me then
in a way I did not want?
Did I betray you there?

Do not think of it!
Past tenses
They question me
these women loved.
I have sometimes thought
Would not life with a woman somewhere
have been a better life, releasing
My denial,
fathering children?
I could be a good
Father. I love children
and they love me.
Their innocence sees
my love. I do love them
yet I have denied myself
and some good woman
a children future, perhaps.
Is something
betrayed here?

There are shadows here
And yet
Denial is just the naive
suppression of the desire
not to acknowledge.
And I have known myself
too well, not to embrace the shadows
that show up light
and truth. Should I enter
such shadows
now?

Think only of my men. Between us
there is no betrayal.
All that is between
us is the love we have had
and the covenant shared
tonight. Men I love you
in the special love
way of men together, men
friends in the knowing,

in the physical
being a man, loved
like a Father knows a Son,
different (but precious yet)
from a daughter. And
All allowed, of course,
this men knowing, allowed
by the rule makers,
religious markers,
right declarers;
love seeming uncomplicated
by lure, sex
not raising a head.

But deep down
I know that
For me there has been beauty
in the men, in the strong
stripped arm of the fisherman,
in their bright, calculating
eye, and more, so much more.

But with my men
and the women
I will say nothing
on these things.
Others may
read what they will
into my silence,
may even try
to make it mean
what they want it to mean.
For myself I leave
only a mystery
to be explored, not defined,
and turn only to those
who wayt with me
Now

I look at the three
men I shared the cup with
tonight and see
into their hearts
and know their desires.
I look into my own heart
and see

James there, my beloved disciple,
my practical man.
And I know what you want, James.
You want the practice
continuing, preached faith
shown in works
demonstration in acts
of ready charity. And your concern
is mine. Not for you sucking
to the rich, regarding money
as the right
to privilege.
And I love you
for this sight.
You with me
have seen light
in poor faces
In the crowd
picking out the God
love favours in the broken.

They sign dependence
as a way to see
Truth; expose the
need for charity
we all need.
And with me James
you have seen
these things and so
you have always wanted
the hungry fed
and bread for them.

You were there
the first time
I broke bread.
Do you not remember that?
I broke the bread
on the hillside and fed
cran full. And how we laughed,
laughed at the bread
joke and giving it away.
And how they hated that
those "wise" ones.
"Something for nothing!
Ought not to be allowed!"
they said through
the laughter of the crowd,
the raising of the bowed,
the crying out loud
looks of surprise
patterns in eyes.
What a day that was.
Just to think of it
fills my cup of happiness again.
Drink in the memory!

But was betrayal there too?
Did I give you a hope
I cannot match
in pursuing another hope?
I could feed crowds again,
I know it.
I could go to you now
and hear your voice say
"Do it!" and want
to with all my heart
but I am afraid
of your practical voice,
its question
marks me for
you do not understand
my nature
in the bread.

I am afraid
to say it, but even as
you want the physical fed
I want to give another
type of bread.
My giving bread
is always a sign
saying, spiritual
hunger's may be satisfied,
though bodies always ask
for more.

But might there always be those
who betray my desire to say
that giving is not enough,
that change is required also.
When only part of my way
is claimed, there is betrayal.
So James, does my betray
of your false hope
in me, make you turn away
tonight?

And what of you,
loved poet John?
I see you, brother,
over there
With me
you have seen
some of the wonder
in creation.
You remember
the wedding
watering the wine
to make the celebration
run strong.
When I filled the jars
brimful with astonishment
at the miracle, faced wonder
full of feteing.
They called that wine
the best and drank

cups of joy
full new wine.
You tasted that
water in the cup
become wine and now
you want to weave
that wonder into poem words.
Did you once find words hard?
Did that create you bard?

John, there is something
of the poet in me.
For I love the words
as you love them
now, and part of me wants
the wine you want
by the skinful
for there must be joy
there must be celebration
and this is what you dream of
in your dreams of me.
But poet? Have you not seen
that mine is not old
wine to confine
in tight containers
of things past.
John, there is only a new
wine covenant cup.
Miracles belong with festival
Do you now desire miracle
without feast day?
Do you want wonder —
working without celebration
when I have never gone
That wonder working way?
Poets do betray
in the struggle
for words and wonder.

I know that
dreams not rooted
in the reality of struggle

are seed sown in the sand
and words from shallow dreams
are sand blown to the wind.
Joy is wonder
through pain, and celebration
that seeks only wonder
is sensation without meaning.

And I can always be betrayed
when you want to turn
my life into only lovely
liturgy of words not work,
engaging hearts but not living?
Will part of my betrayal be
when you start making me
only pretty pretty
when really I am marred
with human being scarred
that is more beautiful by far?

John, is it possible then
that you turn away?
Are there, seeds
for your betray?

And what of you my other love man,
while the thunder brothers rumble,
you Simon, bumble around
so much of the time
not really understanding
I named you Rock,
my little joke,
but true to build on.
You bring another accumulation
of memory.
Unlike some of my other men
you were not jealous
when the Sons of Thunder
brothers stormed
me with their demands
to be kingdom men,

for you have always been
sure of your place,
stubborn in your protection
of me. Ever since the first
calling when I said, "Be
a different sort of fisherman and you wandered in
to following me, making me
appease the wife you were
leaving with the mother-
in-law healing.

Bless you Simon.
You declared me "Anointed One"
when others questioned
and perhaps I questioned too,
"Who do people say that I am?"
But when you said "Anointed"
you wanted my calling
on your terms, I see that
now, raising my suppressed
Satan, making me afraid
of your protection.
You are raising that demon
again now as I watch you.
Old temptations, I thought
put away stir up inside me
again. So many times I have tried
to show you another way.
I washed your feet
and you wanted me lifted up.
"You will not wash my feet!"
you said. I insisted
and you wanted more,
and again I had to deny
your blind obedience.

And now, you have the power
sword at your side
and you are ready again
to swing at what you believe
to be my enemy,

just as tonight around the cup
you declared your ... what?
Belief? Trust? Allegance?
"Everyone else may lose faith
but I will not," you said.
And I knew you were betrayer
there, for yours is the subtlest
of tests, your devotion betrays me
into betrayal of my choice
to give my power away.
Before the cock crows
twice, you, my stubborn devotee,
will have betrayed me three
times. That I see.
And I will have betrayed
your hope in me,
the hope that I should be
some kind of earth Lord
leader of you earth men.

But I cannot be that admired
Lord, to give you unquestioned
devotion in my service.
I cannot be the Lord who takes away
the questions, who tells you what is true
for blind obedience.
I cannot give you freedom
if you cage yourself
to what you want me
to tell you to do.
All I give is responsibility
and the right
to be wrong sometimes
in the decisions you make.

And yet there, I see,
I can also be betrayed.
They might want to call me "Lord",
as you have wanted Simon,
to make my words infallible

and justify their cause,
not mine. They may even call me
"Majesty" or "King"
so that they may fight for
war in those false names.
And they will be wrong
and I will be betrayed
when they pick up weapons
of word or wood or worse
and link them to my name
for there they will deny
my truth, that love only is a way.

And there we have it,
in each of the hearts of my closest
the essence of Betray,
a kind of truth.
I seem to have communicated
Nothing, even to these my heart men.
Look at them. They sleep.
Sunk into darkness and dreaming.
Wake up. Wake up men.
Could none of you stay awake, even
this time? Wake up and pray
that you might be spared
the test of your betray.
Will you see what is happening
in your hearts as well
as your heads.
In your spirits
you are with me
but the weak flesh traps you
with earth things.
You are turning away.

And Judas has turned.
I see that now.
Disciple Judas, you went away
from my bread breaking,
did not want the cup taking.
But turn from bread and wine
and you turn away from me,

For This is all I have.
Turning away Judas,
you enact the betrayal of them all.

Perhaps the cleverest
of my disciples, you have seen
through me. The others have not yet seen
my betrayals of their false hopes
in me, but you have seen
and in this seeing, you now see me
as betrayer of a way to be betrayed.
And now you love the cause
you thought I was
enough to betray.
You have gone into the shadows
to make ready for your way
not mine. In this garden,
betrayal comes again.
In this night you are awake
but sleep to my truth, alive
you move towards death.

And for us
Death is

everything. It is weep
in the eyes of the child, the dark
night of the soul; it is
sand covering the footprint,
the justification of the drunkard,
reason to the suicide,
a final affront to meaning,
the last gasp of the absurd,
a last laugh at love,
the destruction of all that is
creative, a separation
from all that has been
known until now. It is
extinguishing the light,
going into night. Summing up
whatever has gone before,

it confronts the present
with loss and the future
with nothing but grief
for those who remain
to defy. To take death
is to give blank, to make tragic,
to cry tears, to claim the cruel
truth that the more we love,
the more we grieve the loved ones

Death. We hurry through life
to achieve and death denies
it all. For some there may be monuments
for later generations. They mean nothing.
They are only vain attempts to proclaim
a grandeur that the death
mock denies always.
Simon wanted monuments, once
upon a hillside but
I have always denied
such monuments. But
do I tonight, when
the cup presented
seems the death cup?

And I do not want to die!
I do not want to die.

Oh PapaGod, take the cup from me!
I have given, these years,
only a way of love service.
Does love service always
end in death?

I do not want to die.

I have loved you, Judas
as I loved my other men.
Ah Judas, what have I done to you?
How have I offended you? Answer me?

As all the others
I have loved you too.
Loved? Is my love now past tense
now I know your way,
does my love for you cease?
What says the love I have
lived with these times?
What does the prayer
answer? What could love be
in this present

tense? If I went from this place
I could escape from your future
plans, Judas. I could save
myself. That way I could take
your betrayal and betray it.
I could leave
the denying Now
Go away.

And why should I not just go?
Not to go seems to deny everything
I have ever done. It puts Question
over every last story
I have told, makes the health I have
brought come to death too.
Going would let me continue
for a while the good
things I have begun.
And should I deny myself
more opportunities to speak
and leave only silence
where a new word might be?
There are more words
to say, perhaps
I could even help you Judas
see the error in your way,
with more and deeper explanation.
I could run from here
now. Not let you betray
me Judas. That would give you a chance
to think again. Could time open

your eyes? Why should I not just go?
Give me and you Judas
more time, together,
to make a new now
that might-be future.
If I remain I will have more time.
Death will be have to be faced
again in the future
Why not face it in tomorrow's
time? Perhaps I could have
more courage then.

But time is betrayed
when we want more of it.
Time is human creation.
For God, the whole is now,
and Truth is, I see it,
if time is human
and God is now,
then the moment of dying
matters only to that Now.
Turning time into tomorrow
betrays today,
refusing life now in the hope
of some kind of compensation,
is not my way.
Pie in the sky
always tastes stale,
for those who want tomorrow's bread
must eat today.
Must I accept the betray?

Yet even as I think of this
there appears another way.

Though I have always
known myself betrayed
by those who run away
by those who refuse
to take my truth
seriously, by those

who would turn my love
into dogma, truth into tradition,
action into words about action,
The question now put to me
says, Why should I not run away?

Perhaps I should just go
into the silence. Take myself
into an exile, a long way
from here. If all I have
done until now is create
such a confusion
of betrayals even in those
I have loved the most
then should I not renounce
the confusion and go and make
a new quiet start someplace
where I interfere in lives no more
Wait for the moment and
my men would never know
if I were to go.

I could just disappear,
leave nothing but a memory
of something half hoped for
perhaps. They could talk
about me, and our time together
into their futures.
Such a quiet escape
is the way legends arise.
This way I could
have a future too,
a new future to be explored
not caught up in my past.
I could leave it all
behind. Have I not done enough?
Why not just go?
Perhaps I should just
Banish myself
from this garden,
leave the cup for another
to pick up.

There would be pain
of separation; there might
be a way of sacrifice
without death in this way.
I have talked of love
sacrifice, sometimes,
and the need to give yourself
away. Would not this way
deny myself for them,
a way of renouncing
without the need for death?
And does not this going way,
protect the betrayer
from his betray?
Does love not seek the good
for a friend or enemy?
If I stay Judas, do I not
make you my enemy.
But to renounce myself
in a mystery of escape
could that not be loves answer?

And for my other disciples —
To go would stop
me leaving you the guilt
of your betrayals.
If I stay you will wish
you had done something
different, said something
another way. If I take
betrayal, I leave you
pain, and nothing else;
all other possibilities
will go. If I take the
death cup, I leave you
grief — you will grieve
for yourselves.

Oh my disciples
can you tell me what I should do?

Shall I go
and protect you
from your betrayals
and from death?

If I could wake you
from your sleeping now
would you not want that too?
You would not see me hurt
would you my friends?

See, PapaGod, They are loyal
at least! They do not
want my death, do they?

So PapaGod, take the cup from me!
Let me save
myself. I am your Child
and it is too much
to bear, to take death
for myself,
no more possibilities,
no more time,
and leave guilt, pain
and grief for my friends
Let me go from this

But if I go — as I know I can —
would I then not betray myself
and my hopes
for some kind of kingdom
in which even death has its place?
Has not everything I have done
until now been death defying?
Did I not bring dead laws to light,
bring dead eyes to sight,
raise the Lazarite?
I sense
in the subtleties
of these betrayals

the return of my shadow
Satan inside.
The betrayals of my disciples
take me in ways I have conquered
before. Take more time
prompts my desire
for personal power,
for the miracles to continue.
Run from here, says it is possible
to do the impossible thing
and escape from myself,
and my way.

Take this cup from me....

and yet all the while
this is the cup I have taken
to drink from. Until now
all I have offended
with my way have been
the Scribes and Pharisees,
but now my way causes offence
to friends shall I abandon it?
Is there a deeper way to conquer
than the run away?

Can I not conquer
the betrayal by claiming it.

If I love their betrayal
does that not transform it
to my way? If I love
the grief I leave them with
might that not give them
back the love that prompts
the grief? If I claim the death
their betrayal leaves me with
might that not conquer the guilt
of their betrayal, when they see
me take their guilt

in my love embrace, guilt
offering a true
love sacrifice of giving.

If I pour my blood into my loving
cup, will not even death be
pass over, old testament become new
testament, "when I see the blood
I will passover them"
in a new way.

Love your enemies,
I said once. Is death
not also an enemy
to be loved.
So if I put up my lips
and kiss death
full in the face
with love..... what then?
Can I kill death
in claiming it?
Would this not make me conquerer?
Might not such a kiss conquer
all the dead ways?

So prayer takes
the suffering
and in its longing
for the simple
the cup comes back.
I see it does PapaGod.
The intimacy of the true child
prayer is restored.
I become
a new kind of child
in this seeing.

I see this
is not an easy
way. I am still afraid of it.

It asks I put the sweat
of my fear and blood
into my cup and change
into red ring of courage,
part given, part taken.

These things are truth
and the final consequence
of the decisions I have
made. And so I say,
PapaGod, not my false will
to run away, but your
will be done in my willing
submission to your will way.
As before I claim
and love the decisions
and the death
for life.

In this green
garden, I will
be faithful
to the end,
and the life
I see here
will continue
to be life
but all so new,
for the garden
seeing death
sees also new
creation.
It groans with dying, yet
the dying is a way
to life.

And the dark place
gives way to the day
place. And from the darkness
of this night
of death, I begin to see

the colours creating
day again, their rainbow,
and more. I see a new son
rising, blood red
from morning, Blues
away to the heavens; I begin
to smell the perfume
as dry earth after rain
promises life again.
I pluck the olive and taste it
I take the grape
and anticipate the wine.

I will not run
away. I will claim the life
I have lived
and live each remaining now,
I shall suffer,
I know but the suffering
sacrifice and death
will be embraced.
I will take all
their joy and suffering
knowing that
at the heart of joy
is the sadness that joy
will not last for ever,
and that
at the heart
of sadness is
the joy that created it.

I shall die
in the body,
and part of me
remains afraid
of these things.
But into death now
I pour all I have been,
am, will be.
Here I carry to the Papagod
the chaos and confusion

of all the dying,
the tragedies of life
cut short in accident
or deliberate intent
and the sins personal
Satans corrupt in life.

I claim death to conquer
and carry all
the dying who have the courage
to die with me.
I will take the cup,
even to the point
of appearing drunk
on it and in taking it
I will offer some kind of hope
as true sacrifice.
In all this I may become
a mystery to many,
a mystery of one embracing
the mystery of death.
Now I take only the way
of silent acceptance
of that Will
Be.

Look! Look!
Here comes the awe-ful
dead kiss.
My disciples you sleep
still. But now you must wake to me!
My time has come.
Betrayal in all its forms
is upon me
to be betrayed
and I shall meet

Everything.
I shall do
Enough!
Nearly,
it is finished.